BRAIN
TRAINING
PUZZLES

— QUICK BOOK 2 —

THIS IS A CARLTON BOOK

Published by Carlton Books Limited
20 Mortimer Street
London W1T 3JW

ISBN 978-1-84732-200-5

Printed in China

BRAIN
TRAINING
PUZZLES

— QUICK BOOK 2 —

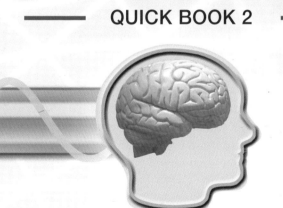

Introduction

Welcome to brain-training. You are probably here because you don't want to lose any more grey cells, or because you think your brain is getting old, or because your memory isn't what it used to be, or maybe simply because you like puzzles. The good news, whatever your reason for picking up this book, is that if you solve a lot of puzzles you'll be exercising your brain. As with your body, you need to give your brain some exercise to keep it healthy. But remember – looking after your brain isn't just a case of exercise and keeping the cells topped up with water like your car battery – get enough sleep, keep your stress level low and watch what you eat. Strange advice from a puzzle book indeed, but if you really care about your brain you'll look into all of those things – but don't forget to enjoy yourself!

And that brings us back to the puzzles in this book. There are many different types and you can solve them in any order you choose. The best way is to tackle a few puzzles a day and work your way through steadily. If you get stuck, just move on and try a different one; you'll probably find that the one that had you fretting for hours will be easy when you come back to it.

Don't give up, have fun, and above all enjoy!

Spot the Difference

Can you spot ten differences between this pair of pictures?

Answer on page 157

Masyu

Draw a single unbroken line around the grid that passes through all the circles. The line must enter and leave each box in the centre of one of its four sides.

Black Circle: Turn left or right in the box, and the line must pass straight through the next and previous boxes.

White Circle: Travel straight through the box, and the line must turn in the next and/or previous box.

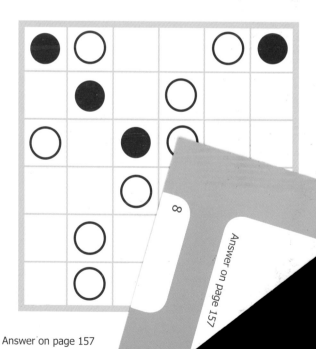

8

Answer on page 157

Answer on page 157

All Change

The colours of each triangle in pattern B is directly related to the colours in pattern A. Can you apply the same the rules and fill in pattern C?

A

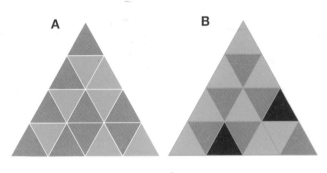

B

C

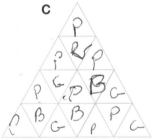

Bits and Pieces

Can you match the four halves of broken plate?

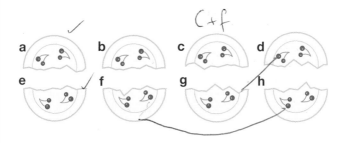

Answer on page 157

9

Boxes

Playing the game of boxes, each player takes it in turns to join two adjacent dots with a line. If a player's line completes a box, the player wins the box and has another go. It's your turn in the game below. To avoid giving your opponent a lot of boxes, what's your best move?

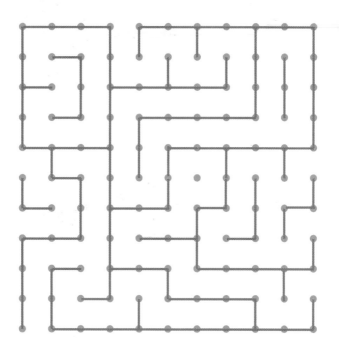

Answer on page 157

Matrix

Which of the boxed figures completes the set?

 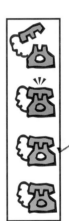

Answer on page 157

Riddle

In my shed at home I have some hamsters and some hamster cages. If I put one hamster in each cage I'd have one hamster too many. But if I put two hamsters in each cage, I'd have one cage left over... How many hamsters and cages have I got?

X (hamster) $= Y - 1$ (hamsters)
cage

$X + 1 = $ no of hamster

Answer on page 157

Can you Cut it?

Cut a straight line through this shape to create two shapes that are identical.

Answer on page 157

Where's the Pair?

Only two of the shapes below are exactly the same, can you find the matching pair?

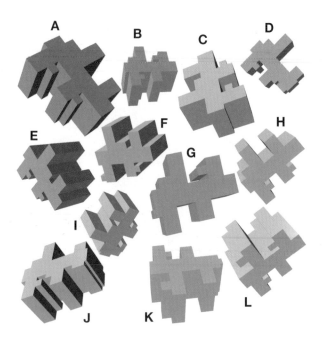

Answer on page 158

Odd Clocks

Buenos Aires is 13 hours behind Melbourne, which is 9 hours ahead of London. It is 12.35 pm on Wednesday in Melbourne – what time is it in the other two cities?

MELBOURNE

LONDON

BUENOS AIRES

Answer on page 158

Sudoku

Complete the grid so that the numbers 1, 2, 3, 4, 5, 6, 7, 8 and 9 appear once only in each row, column and 9x9 square.

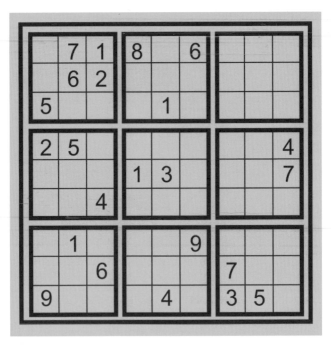

Answer on page 158

Sudoku

Complete the grid so that the numbers 1, 2, 3, 4, 5, 6, 7, 8 and 9 appear once only in each row, column and 9x9 square.

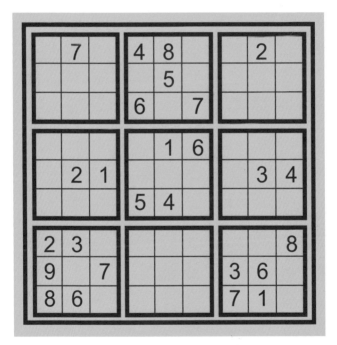

Answer on page 158

Sudoku

Complete the grid so that the numbers 1, 2, 3, 4, 5, 6, 7, 8 and 9 appear once only in each row, column and 9x9 square.

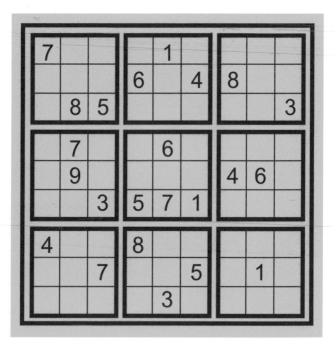

Answer on page 158

Sudoku

Complete the grid so that the numbers 1, 2, 3, 4, 5, 6, 7, 8 and 9 appear once only in each row, column and 9x9 square.

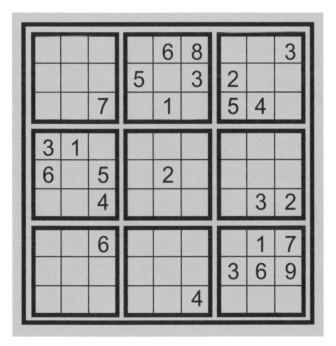

Answer on page 158

Riddle

On this island in the middle of a lake, there is a tractor, used in summer to give tourists rides around the place. The tractor didn't get there by boat or by air, and it wasn't built there either... so how did it get there?

Answer on page 158

Arrows

Complete the grid by drawing an arrow in each box that points in any one of the eight compass directions (N, E, S, W, NE, NW, SE, SW). The numbers in the outside boxes in the finished puzzle will reflect the number of arrows pointing in their direction.

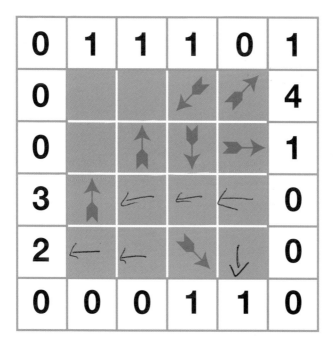

Answer on page 158

Checkers

Make a move for white so that eight black pieces are left, none of which are in the same column or row.

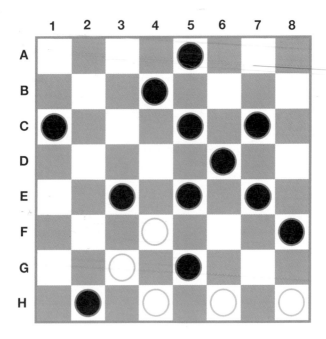

Answer on page 159

Cube Route

Can you crack the colour code and make your way from one red square to the other? Each colour takes you up, down, left or right. The blue arrow tells you which way is up...

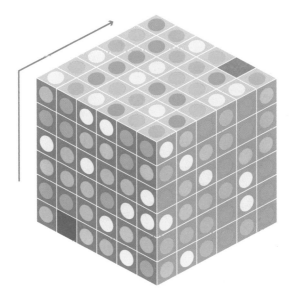

Green =
Pink =
Yellow =
Orange =

Answer on page 159

Cut and Fold

Which of the Patterns below is created by this fold and cut?

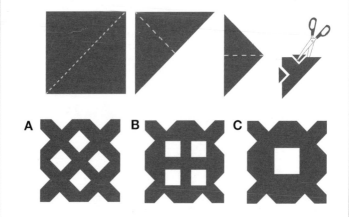

A

B

C

Answer on page 159

Double Drat

All these shapes appear twice in the box except one. Can you spot the singleton?

Answer on page 159

Game of Two Halves

Which two shapes below will pair up to create the top shape?

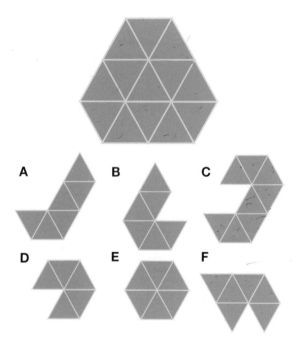

A   B   C

D   E   F

Answer on page 159

Get the Picture

These two grids, when merged together, will make a picture...
Of what?

Answer on page 159

Gridlock

Which square correctly completes the grid?

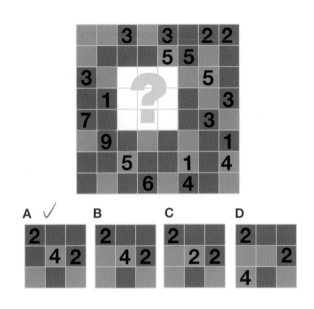

A ✓

B

C

D

Answer on page 159

Location

Below is an altered view of a world-famous landmark. Can you tell where it is?

Answer on page 159

Masyu

Draw a single unbroken line around the grid that passes through all the circles. The line must enter and leave each box in the centre of one of its four sides.

Black Circle: Turn left or right in the box, and the line must pass straight through the next and previous boxes.

White Circle: Travel straight through the box, and the line must turn in the next and/or previous box.

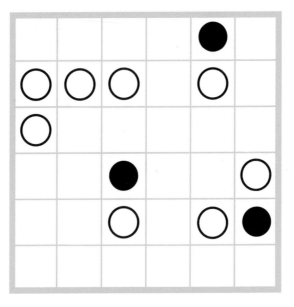

Answer on page 160

Mini Nonogram

The numbers by each row and column describe black squares and groups of black squares that are adjoining. Colour in all the black squares and a six number combination will be revealed.

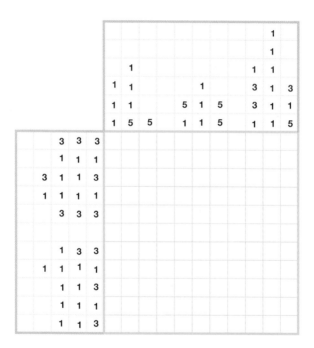

Answer on page 160

Mirror Image

Only one of these pictures is an exact mirror image of the first one? Can you spot it?

Answer on page 160

Odd One Out

Which of the shapes below is not the same as the other ones?

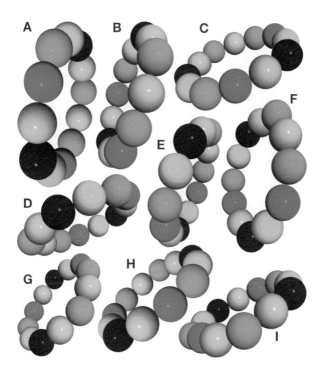

Answer on page 160

Patch of the Day

Place the shape over the grid so that no colour appears twice in the same row or column. Beware, the shape may not be the right way up!

Answer on page 160

Picture Parts

Which box contains exactly the right bits to make the pic?

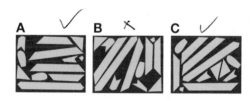

A ✓   B ✗   C ✓

Answer on page 160

Where's the Pair?

Only two of these pictures are exactly the same.
Can you spot the matching pair?

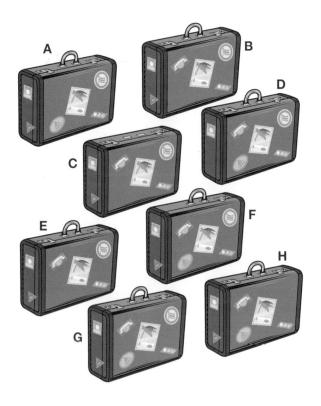

Answer on page 160

Sum Total

Replace the question marks with mathematical symbols (+, −, × or ÷) to make a working sum.

$$22 \; ? \; 8 \; ? \; 5 \; ? \; 3 = 3$$

14 − 5 9

30

22 + 8 ÷ 5

30   6 − 3 = 3

Answer on page 160

Spot the Difference

Can you spot ten differences between this pair of pictures?

Answer on page 161

Sum People

Work out what number is represented by which person and replace the question mark.

14

20

26

23

?   24   12   30

Answer on page 161

Shape Shifting

Fill in the empty squares so that each row, column and long diagonal contains five different symbols

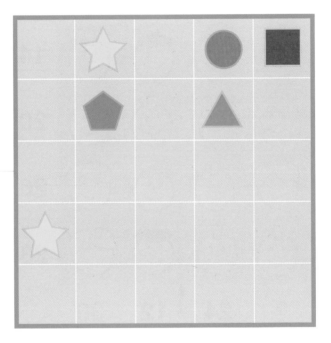

Answer on page 161

Scene It?

The four squares below can all be found in the picture grid, can you track them down? Beware, they may not be the right way up!

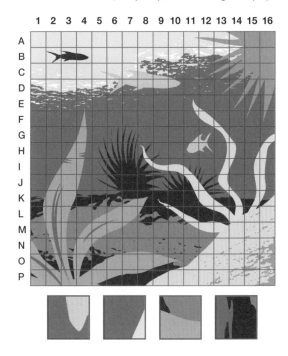

Answer on page 161

Shape Shifting

Fill in the empty squares so that each row, column and long diagonal contains six different symbols.

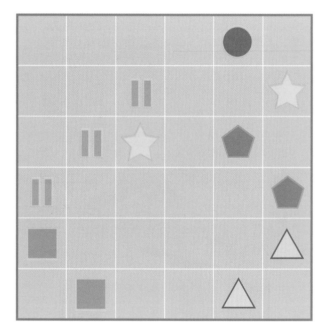

Answer on page 161

Pots of Dots

How many dots should there be in the hole in this pattern?

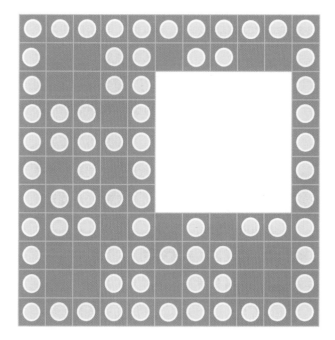

Answer on page 161

Piece Puzzle

Only one of these pieces fits the hole in our main picture – the others have all been altered slightly by our artist. Can you place the missing pic?

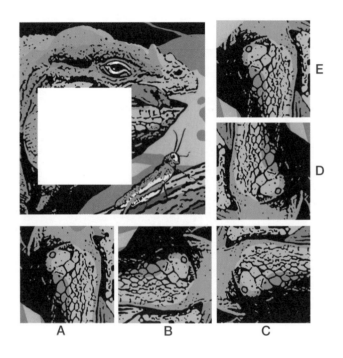

Answer on page 161

44

Number Mountain

Replace the question marks with numbers so that each pair of blocks adds up to the block directly above them.

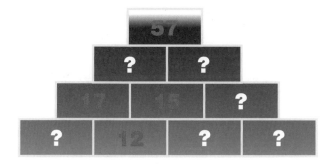

Answer on page 161

View From Above

Of the plan views below, only one of them is a true overhead representation of the scene shown here – can you work out which?

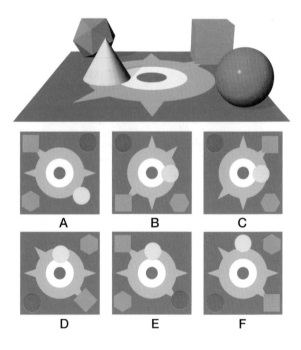

Answer on page 162

Block Party

Assuming all blocks that are not visible from this angle are present,
how many blocks have been removed from this 5 × 5 × 5 cube?

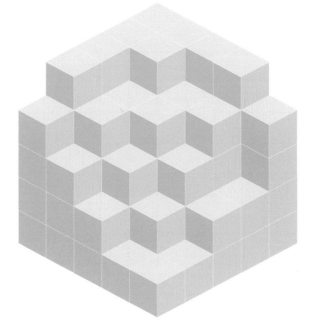

Answer on page 162

Boxes

Playing the game of boxes, each player takes it in turns to join two adjacent dots with a line. If a player's line completes a box, the player wins the box and has another go. It's your turn in the game below. To avoid giving your opponent a lot of boxes, what's your best move?

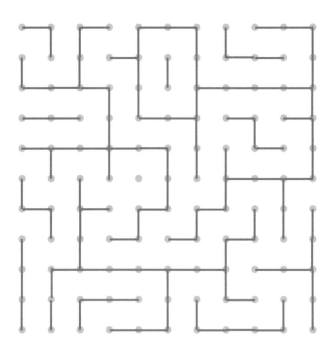

Answer on page 162

Camp Conifer

Every tree 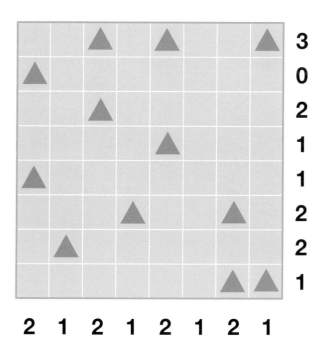 has one tent found horizontally or vertically adjacent to it. No tent can be in an adjacent square to another tent (even diagonally). The numbers by each row and column tell you how many tents are there. Can you locate all the tents?

Cats and Cogs

Turn the handle in the indicated direction... Does the cat go up or down?

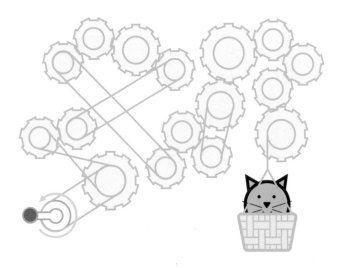

Answer on page 162

Cube Route

Can you crack the colour code and make your way from one red square to the other? Each colour takes you up, down, left or right. The blue arrow tells you which way is up...

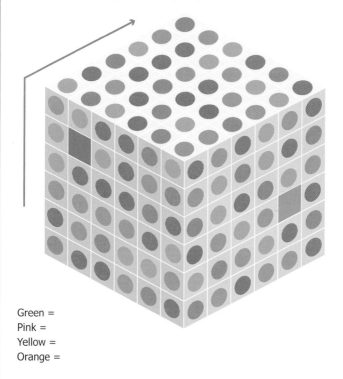

Green =
Pink =
Yellow =
Orange =

Answer on page 162

Cut and Fold

Which of the patterns below is created by this fold and cut?

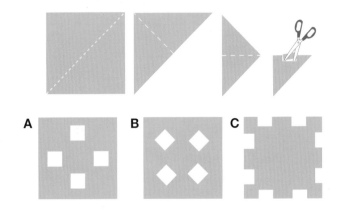

A

B

C

Answer on page 162

Scene It?

The four squares below can all be found in the picture grid – can you track them down? Beware, they may not be the right way up!

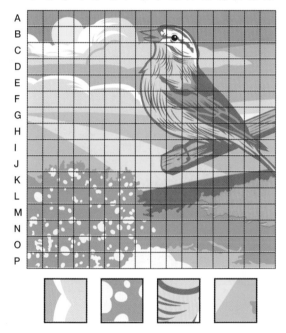

Answer on page 162

Riddle

When the new hospital was built, Big Dave was hired to paint the numbers 1 to 100 on the rooms. How many times will Dave be painting the number 9?

Answer on page 163

Rainbow Reckoning

The art gallery is being redecorated. The rooms will be either brown, yellow or pink, and no two adjacent rooms can be the same colour. What colour will the conservatory be?

Answer on page 163

Sum Total

Replace the question marks with mathematical symbols (+, −, × or ÷) to make a working sum.

$$8 ? 3 ? 6 ? 2 = 8$$

Answer on page 163

Where's the Pair?

Only two of these pictures are exactly the same. Can you spot the matching pair?

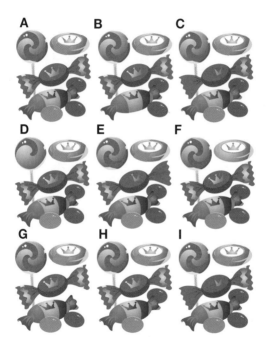

A

B

C

D

E

F

G

H

I

Answer on page 163

Which Wheel?

Which of the wheels, a, b, c, or d, is missing from the set below?

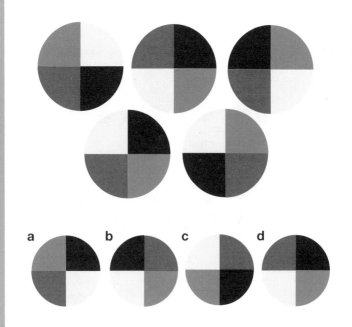

Answer on page 163

Spot the Difference

Can you spot ten differences between this pair of pictures?

Answer on page 163

Odd Clocks

Karachi is 4 hours ahead of Paris, which is 8 hours behind Tokyo. It is 9.05 pm on Thursday in Paris – what time is it in the other two cities?

PARIS

TOKYO **KARACHI**

Answer on page 163

Missing Link

What should replace the question mark so that the grid follows a pattern?

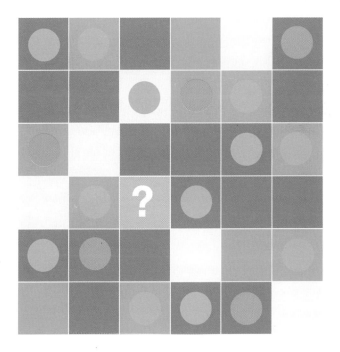

Answer on page 163

Pots of Dots

How many dots should there be in the hole in this pattern?

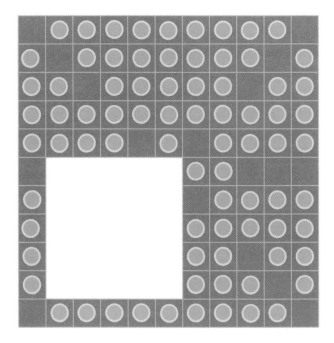

Answer on page 164

Magic Squares

Complete the square using nine consecutive numbers, so that all rows, columns and large diagonals add up to the same total.

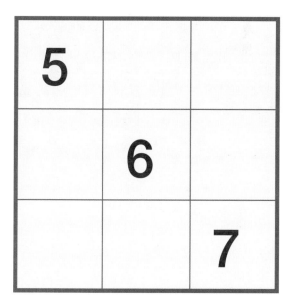

Answer on page 164

Get the Picture

These two grids, when merged together, will make a picture...
Of what?

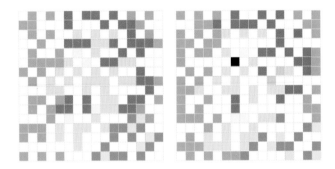

Answer on page 164

Location

Below is an altered view of a world-famous landmark. Can you tell where it is?

Answer on page 164

Riddle

At the auction house, George and Jenna were browsing through the items before the sale began. George had his eye on a ceremonial sword, inscribed to "Captain Beswick Alistair Campbell, for Exceptional Valour in the Field, Belgium, November 12th 1917, WWI". Jenna told him not to be daft, it was forgery! How did she know?

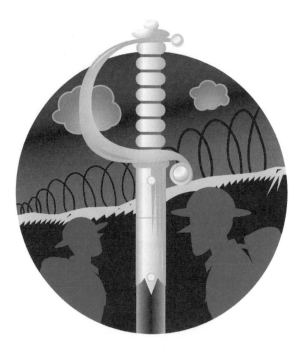

Answer on page 164

View From Above

Of the plan views below, only one of them is a true overhead representation of the scene shown here – can you work out which?

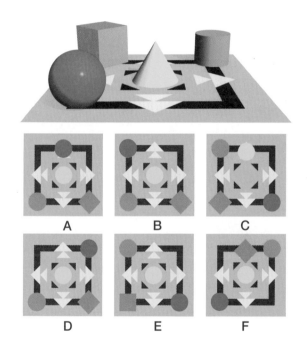

A B C

D E F

Answer on page 164

All Change

The colour of each square in pattern B is directly related to the colours in pattern A. The square colours in pattern C relate to pattern B the same way. Can you apply the same rules and fill in pattern D?

A

B

C

D

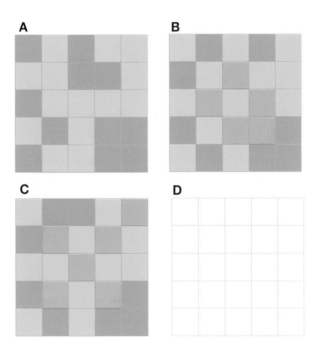

Answer on page 164

Game of Two Halves

Which two shapes below will pair up to create the top shape?

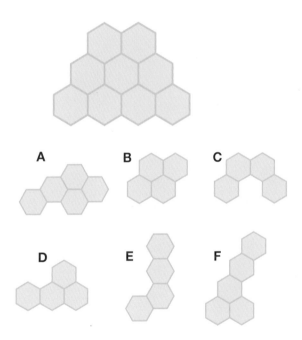

A

B

C

D

E

F

Answer on page 164

Matrix

Which of the boxed figures completes the set?

Answer on page 165

Odd One Out

Which of the shapes below is not the same as the other ones?

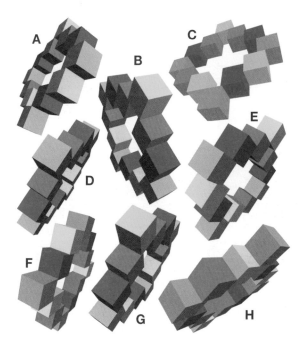

Answer on page 165

Piece Puzzle

Only one of these pieces fits the hole in our main picture – the others have all been altered slightly by our artist. Can you place the missing pic?

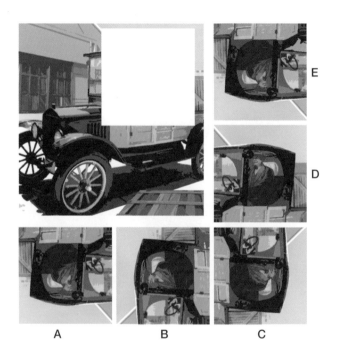

A

B

C

D

E

Answer on page 165

Scene It?

The four squares below can all be found in the picture grid – can you track them down? Beware, they may not be the right way up!

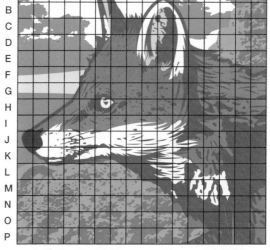

Answer on page 165

Where's the Pair?

Only two of these pictures are exactly the same. Can you spot the matching pair?

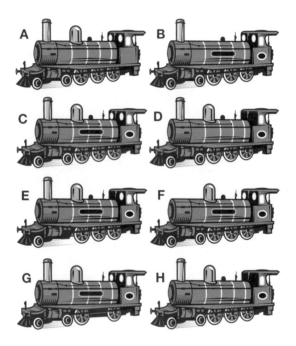

A
B
C
D
E
F
G
H

Answer on page 165

Shape Stacker

Can you work out the logic behind the numbers in these shapes, and the total of A × B?

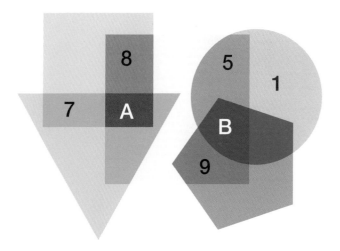

Answer on page 165

Bits and Pieces

Can you match four pieces twice to make two letters of the alphabet?

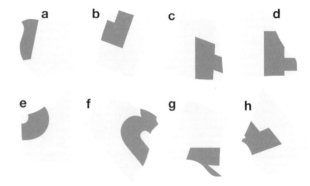

Answer on page 165

Block Party

Assuming all blocks that are not visible from this angle are present, how many blocks have been removed from this 5 × 5 × 5 cube?

Answer on page 165

Sudoku

Complete the grid so that the numbers 1, 2, 3, 4, 5, 6, 7, 8 and 9 appear once only in each row, column and 9x9 square.

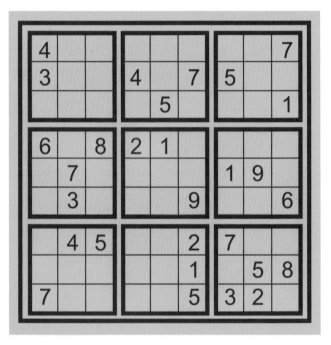

Answer on page 167

Where's the Pair?

Only two of the shapes below are exactly the same – can you find the matching pair?

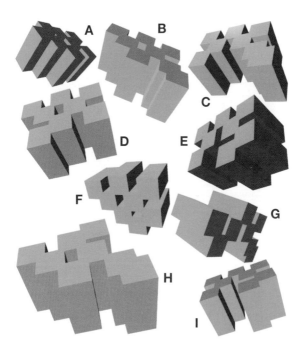

Answer on page 166

Riddle-me-tea

Discovering a fly in my tea, I asked the waiter if he could get me another cup, one without a fly. He came back with my new tea, I tasted it and guess what? The cheeky chancer had given me the same cup of tea back! But how did I know?

Answer on page 166

Matrix

Which of the boxed figures completes the set?

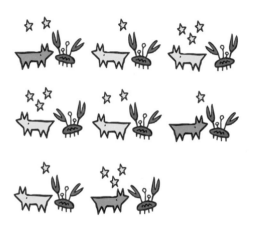

Answer on page 166

Mirror Image

Only one of these pictures is an exact mirror image of the first one? Can you spot it?

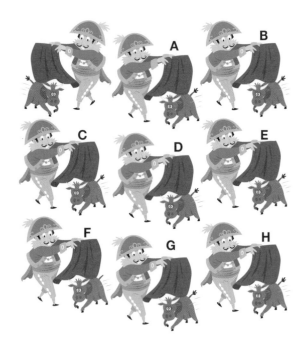

Answer on page 166

Sum Total

Replace the question marks with mathematical symbols (+, −, × or ÷) to make a working sum.

$$10 \; ? \; 2 \; ? \; 4 \; ? \; 7 = 13$$

Answer on page 166

Where's the Pair?

Only two of these pictures are exactly the same. Can you spot the matching pair?

Answer on page 166

Tents and Trees

Every tree 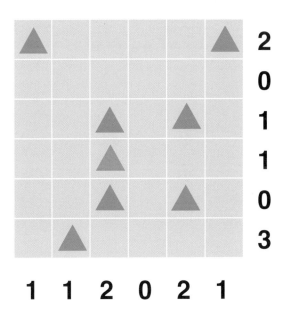 has one tent found horizontally or vertically adjacent to it. No tent can be in an adjacent square to another tent (even diagonally). The numbers by each row and column tell you how many tents are there. Can you locate all the tents?

Answer on page 166

85

Sum Total

Replace the question marks with mathematical symbols (+, −, × or ÷) to make a working sum.

$$14 ? 2 ? 7 ? 1 = 5$$

Answer on page 167

Magic Squares

Complete the square using nine consecutive numbers, so that all rows, columns and large diagonals add up to the same total.

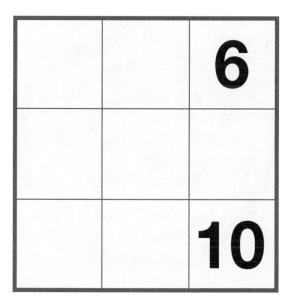

Answer on page 167

Location

Below is an altered view of a world-famous landmark. Can you tell where it is?

Answer on page 167

Matrix

Which of the boxed figures completes the set?

Answer on page 167

Picture Parts

Which box has exactly the right bits to make the pic?

A   **B**   **C**

Answer on page 167

Picture Parts

Which box has exactly the right bits to make the pic?

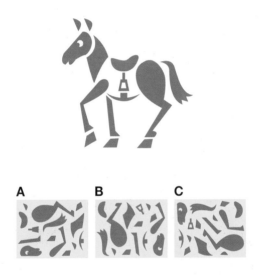

A   **B**   **C**

Answer on page 167

Piece Puzzle

Only one of these pieces fits the hole in our main picture – the others have all been altered slightly by our artist. Can you place the missing pic?

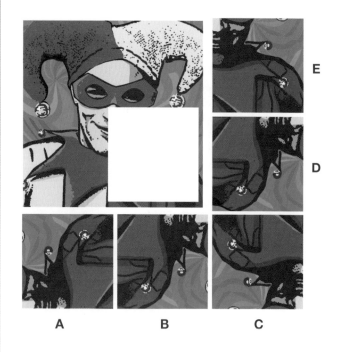

E

D

A   B   C

Answer on page 167

Scene It?

The four squares below can all be found in the picture grid – can you track them down? Beware, they may not be the right way up!

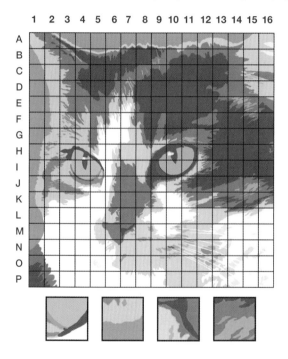

Answer on page 167

Where's the Pair?

Only two of these pictures are exactly the same – can you spot the matching pair?

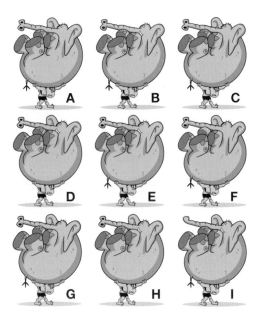

Answer on page 168

Spot the Difference

Can you spot ten differences between this pair of pictures?

Answer on page 168

Riddle

A truck has stopped before a low bridge. The driver is beside himself because the bridge is exactly one inch lower than his truck is high, and this is the only route he can take to his delivery destination. What brilliant plan do you come up with?

Answer on page 168

Box It

The value of each shape is the number of sides each shape has, multiplied by the number within it. Thus a square containing the number 4 has a value of 16. Find a block of four squares (two squares wide by two squares high) with a total value of exactly 50.

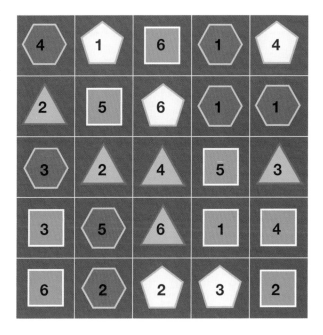

Answer on page 168

Boxes

Playing the game of boxes, each player takes it in turns to join two adjacent dots with a line. If a player's line completes a box, the player wins the box and has another go. It's your turn in the game below. To avoid giving your opponent a lot of boxes, what's your best move?

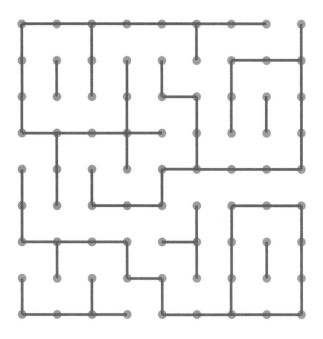

Answer on page 168

Checkers

Make a move for white so that eight black pieces are left, none of which are in the same column or row.

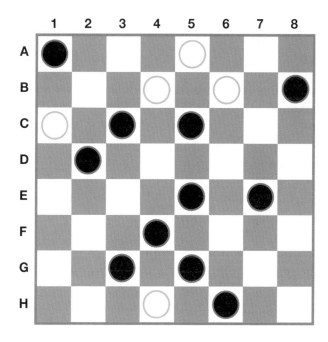

Answer on page 168

Sudoku Six

Complete the first grid so that every row and column contain all the letters GLMRW and Y. Do the same with grid 2 and the numbers 12345 and 6. To decode the finished grid, add the numbers in the shaded squares to the letters in the matching squares in the second (ie: A + 3 = D, Y + 4 = C) to get six new letters which can be arranged to spell the name of a famous composer.

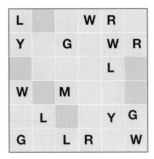

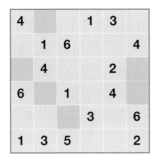

Answer on page 168

Where's the Pair?

Only two of the shapes below are exactly the same – can you find the matching pair?

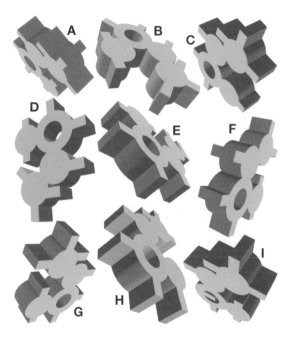

Answer on page 168

Where's the Pair?

Only two of these pictures are exactly the same. Can you spot the matching pair?

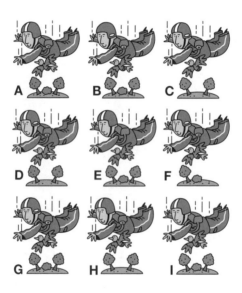

Answer on page 169

Sudoku

Complete the grid so that all rows and columns, and each outlined block of nine squares, contain the numbers 1, 2, 3, 4, 5, 6, 7, 8 and 9.

8		4						9
	2				6		8	
6		9			5			3
			5	7		3	4	8
		3	1					6
4			6				1	
	6	1	9		3			
9		7				2		
			7		4	6		

Answer on page 169

Spot the Difference

Can you spot ten differences between this pair of pictures?

Answer on page 169

Matrix

Which of the boxed figures completes the set?

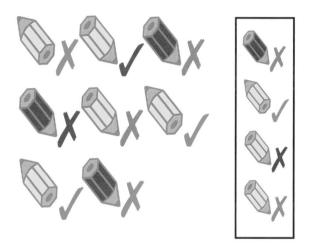

Answer on page 169

Silhouette

Which of the coloured – in pics matches our silhouette?

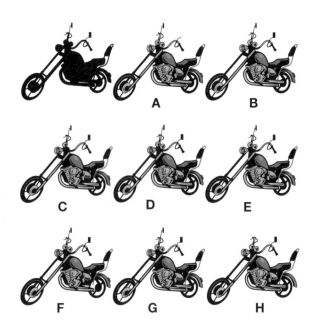

Answer on page 169

X and O

The numbers around the edge of the grid describe the number of X's in the vertical, horizontal and diagonal lines connecting with that square. Complete the grid so that there is an X or O in every square.

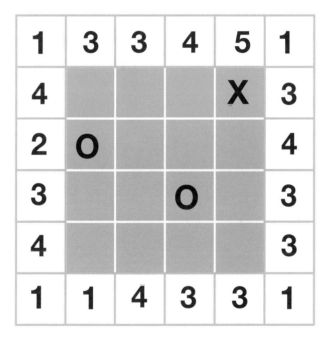

1	3	3	4	5	1
4				X	3
2	O				4
3			O		3
4					3
1	1	4	3	3	1

Answer on page 169

Rainbow Reckoning

This balloon is made up of pink, green and cream panels, with no adjacent panels to be in the same colour. Can you work out what colour the marked panel should be?

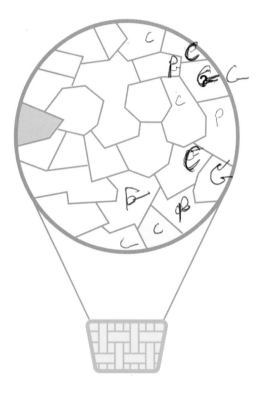

Answer on page 169

Percentage Point

What percentage of this grid is green and what percentage is pink?

$25|12$

13

$\frac{12}{25} \times 100$ 4

48%

52%

Answer on page 169

Missing Link

What should replace the question mark so that the grid follows a pattern?

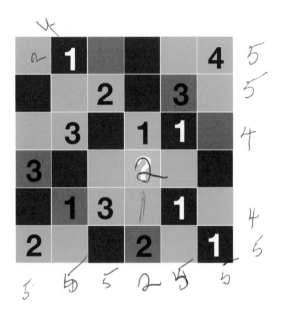

Colour Maze

Find a path from the outside to the inside of the maze. You may only pass from a yellow section to a red one, a red to a purple, a purple to a blue or a blue to a yellow, and you may not travel diagonally.

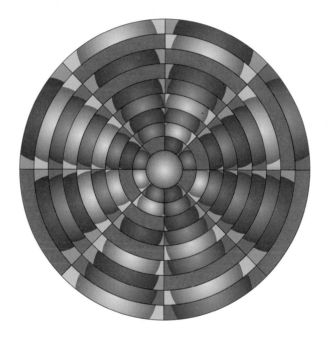

Answer on page 170

Double Maze

Make your way from A to B without passing through any red squares – then do it again without passing through any yellow squares!

Answer on page 170

Get the Picture

These two grids, when merged together, will make a picture...
Of what?

Answer on page 170

Hue Goes There

Three of the sections below can be found in our main grid, one cannot. Can you spot the section that doesn't belong? Beware, the sections might not be the same way round!

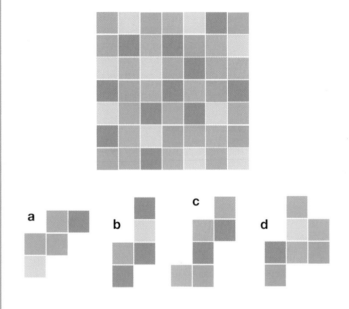

Answer on page 170

Matrix

Which of the boxed figures completes the set?

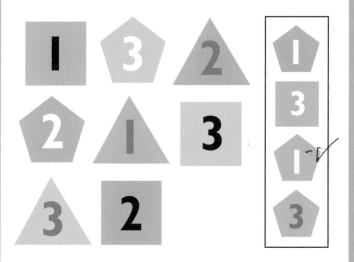

Answer on page 170

Reach for the Stars

Can you find three perfect five-pointed stars in this colourful collection?

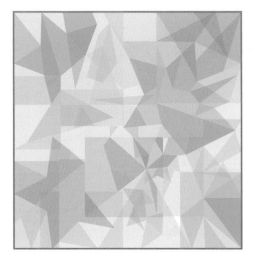

Answer on page 170

Scene It?

The four squares below can all be found in the picture grid – can you track them down? Beware, they may not be the right way up!

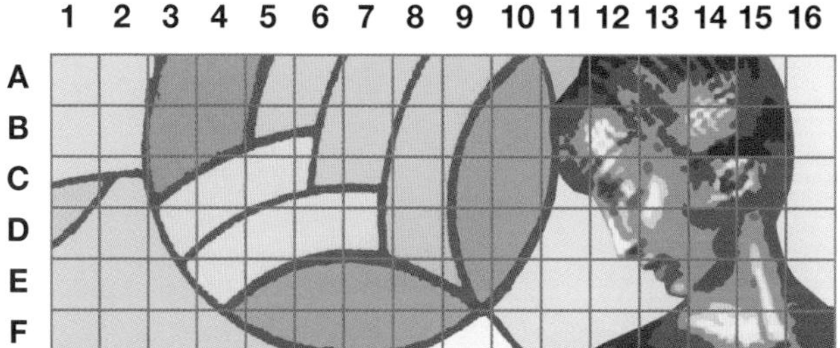

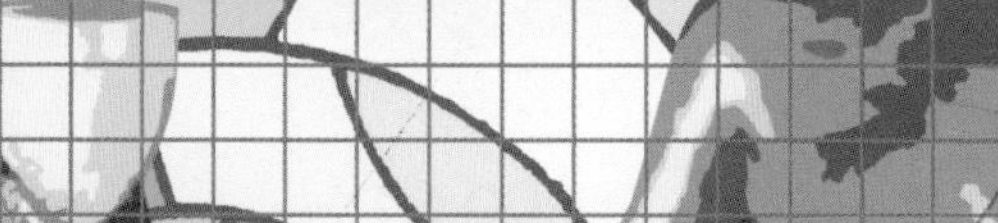

Answer on page 170

(handwritten annotations: B9, L15, N16, G2, 1115, N16)

Odd Clocks

Cairo is 7 hours ahead of Mexico City, which is 5 hours behind Reykjavik. It is 10.30pm on Monday in Mexico City — What time is it in the other two cities?

MEXICO CITY

4.30 am

REYKJAVIK

4.30 pm

CAIRO

Answer on page 171

Latin Square

Complete the grid so that every row and column, and every outlined area, contains the letters A, B, C, D, E and F.

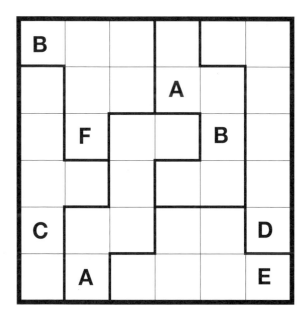

Answer on page 171

Get the Picture

These two grids, when merged together, will make a picture...
Of what?

Answer on page 171

Revolutions

Cog A has 12 teeth, cog B has 8 and cog C has 10. How many revolutions must cog A turn through to bring all three cogs back to these exact positions?

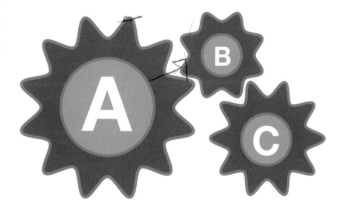

Answer on page 171

Mini Nonogram

The numbers by each row and column describe black squares and groups of black squares that are adjoining. Colour in all the black squares and a six number combination will be revealed.

					5				1					
					1			1	1	5				
				1	1	3		3	1	1		1	1	5
				3	1	1		1	1	3		3	1	5
	1	3	3											
	1	1	1											
	1	1	1											
	1	1	1											
	1	1	1											
3	3	1	1											
1	1	1	1											
	3	3	3											
	1	1	1											
	3	3	1											

Answer on page 171

Odd One Out

Which of the shapes below is not the same as the other ones?

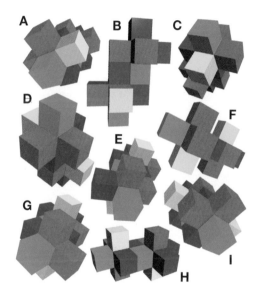

Answer on page 171

Safecracker

To open the safe, all the buttons must be pressed in the correct order before the "open" button is pressed. What is the first button pressed in your sequence?

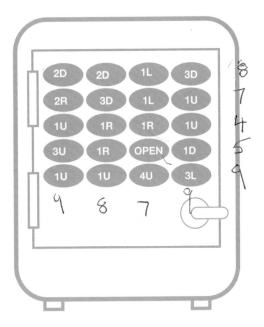

Answer on page 171

Signpost

Can you crack the logical secret behind the distances to these great cities, and work out how far it is to Mumbai?

WARSAW 16

WELLINGTON 27

MUMBAI ?

COLUMBO 18

AMSTERDAM 24

69   27   2W
               2A
              ____
                R
              ____
               16

Answer on page 171

Matrix

Which of the boxed figures completes the set?

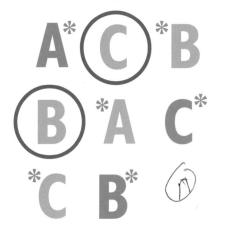

Answer on page 172

Patch of the Day

Place the shape over the grid so that no colour appears twice in the same row or column. Beware, the shape may not be the right way up!

Answer on page 172

Figure it Out

The sequence 6789 can be found once in the grid, reading up, down, backwards, forwards or diagonally. Can you pick it out?

7	6	8	7	6	8	9	8	9	9	8	8
8	7	7	6	7	7	6	6	6	6	6	6
8	8	7	8	8	9	8	9	8	8	9	9
9	7	7	8	8	8	9	7	9	7	8	8
6	6	8	6	7	7	7	8	7	9	7	7
8	9	8	7	8	9	8	9	8	8	7	9
9	8	7	8	9	8	9	6	6	9	8	6
7	8	9	7	6	6	6	8	9	6	6	8
8	6	8	9	8	9	8	9	8	8	9	9
9	9	6	6	9	8	9	8	7	6	7	7
6	7	9	8	6	6	7	8	7	9	8	8
8	9	7	9	8	9	8	9	6	8	9	6

Answer on page 172

Jigsaw

Which three of the pieces below can complete the jigsaw and make a perfect square?

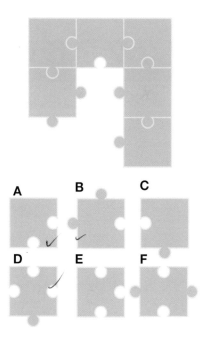

A

B

C

D

E

F

Answer on page 172

Sum Total

Replace the question marks with mathematical symbols (+, −, ×, or ÷) to make a working sum.

$$9 ? 2 ? 2 ? 6 = 20$$

÷ × +

Answer on page 172

Hub Signs

What numbers should appear in the hubs of these number wheels?

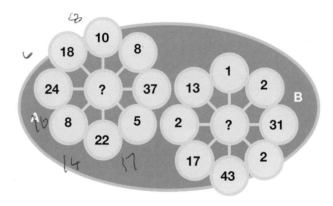

_28_
_24_
_8_
_22_
_6_
_37_
_3_
_125_

_16_
_5_
_37_
_43_
_+0_
_8_

Answer on page 172

Cube Route

Can you crack the colour code and make your way from one purple square to the other? Each colour takes you up, down, left or right. The blue arrow tells you which way is up...

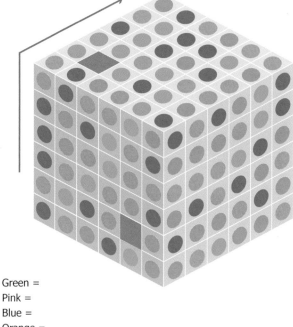

Green =
Pink =
Blue =
Orange =

Answer on page 172

Cut and Fold

Which of the patterns below is created by this fold and cut?

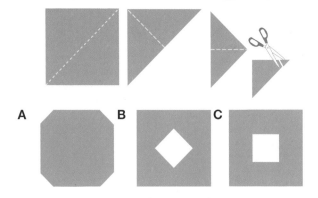

A

B

C

Answer on page 172

Double Drat

All these shapes appear twice in the box except one. Can you spot the singleton?

Answer on page 173

Where's the Pair?

Only two of these pictures are exactly the same. Can you spot the matching pair?

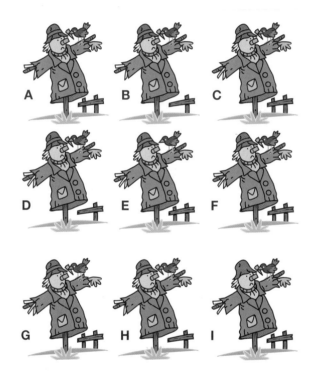

Answer on page 173

Pots of Dots

How many dots should there be in the hole in this pattern?

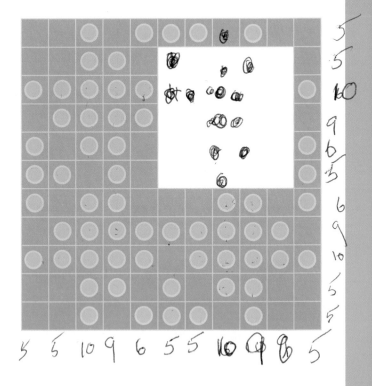

Answer on page 173

Shape Stacker

Can you work out the logic behind the numbers in these shapes, and suggest a number to replace the A and B?

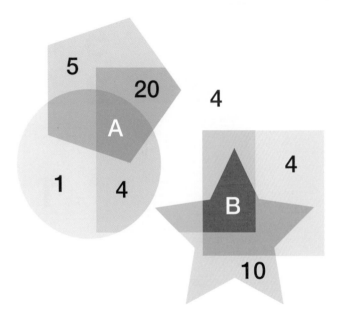

Answer on page 173

Sudoku Sixpack

Complete the grid so that every row, column and long diagonal contains the numbers 1, 2, 3, 4, 5 and 6

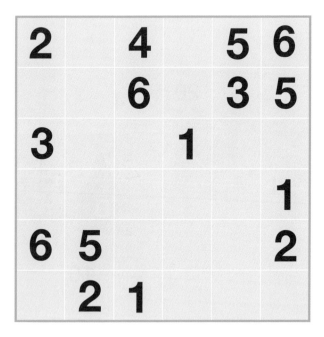

Answer on page 173

Symbol Sums

These symbols represent the numbers 1 to 4. If the red phone represents the number 3, can you work out what the other colour phones are representing and make a working sum?

Tents and Trees

Every tree 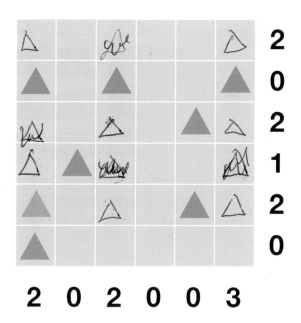 has one tent found horizontally or vertically adjacent to it. No tent can be in an adjacent square to another tent (even diagonally!). The numbers by each row and column tell you how many tents are there. Can you locate all the tents?

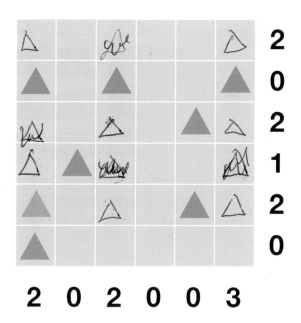

Answer on page 173

Usual Suspects

Sir Lunchalot has his trusty sword and shield, and a red plume on his helmet, which has the visor up. Can you pick him out?

Answer on page 173

Gridlock

Which square correctly completes the grid?

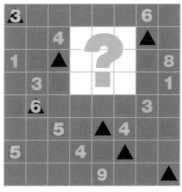

| A | B | C | D |

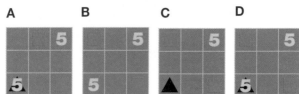

Answer on page 174

Cubism

The shape below can be folded to make a cube. Which of the four cubes pictured below could it make?

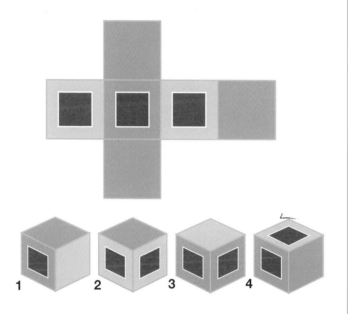

1   2   3   4

Answer on page 174

Game of Two Halves

Which two shapes below will pair up to create the top shape?

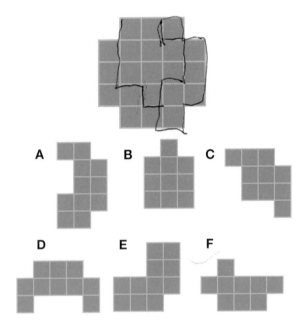

A

B

C

D

E

F

Answer on page 174

Matrix

Which of the boxed figures completes the set?

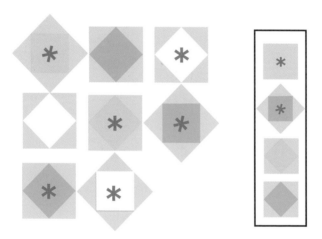

Answer on page 174

More or Less

The arrows indicate whether a number in a box is greater or smaller than an adjacent number. Complete the grid so that all rows and columns contain the numbers 1 to 5.

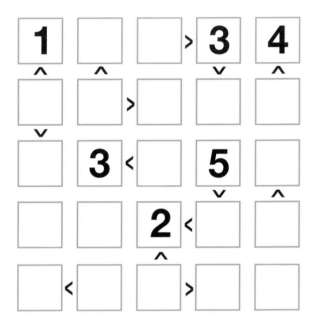

Answer on page 174

Number Sweep

The numbers in some squares in the grid indicate the exact number of shaded squares that should surround it. Colour in the squares until all the numbers are surrounded by the correct number of shaded squares, and a number will be revealed!

	0		0		3			5		2	
0		0		3			8		5		0
	0		3		7			8		3	
0		3		6			8		5		0
	3		6		6	6		8		3	
3				3			8				
				4			8				
	8		6		6	7		8		6	
5		8		8			8		8		5
	5		5				8		6	
2		3		3			8		6		2
	0		0					5		2	

Piece Puzzle

Only one of these pieces fits the hole in our main picture – the others have all been altered slightly by our artist. Can you place the missing pic?

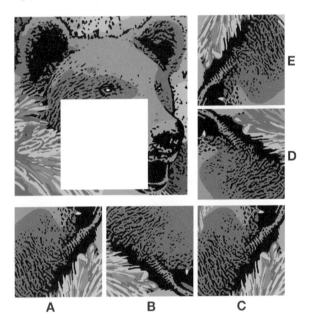

Answer on page 174

Double Maze

Make your way from A to B without passing through any pink squares – then do it again without passing through any purple squares!

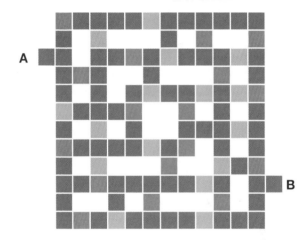

Answer on page 174

Magic Squares

Complete the square using nine consecutive numbers, so that all rows, columns and large diagonals add up to the same total

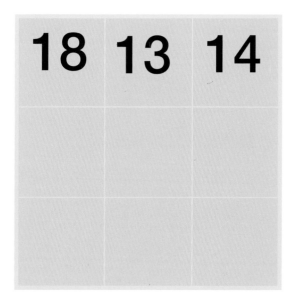

18	13	14

Answer on page 175

Which Wheel?

Which of the wheels, a, b, c, or d, is missing from the set below?

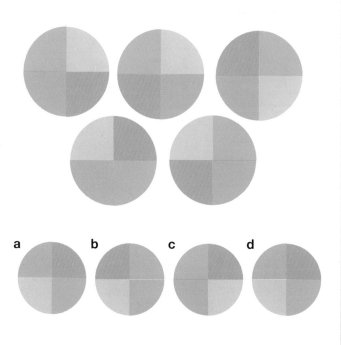

a b c d

Answer on page 175

Symmetry

This picture, when finished, is symmetrical along a vertical line up the middle. Can you colour in the missing squares and work out what the picture is of?

Answer on page 175

Mirror Image

Only one of these pictures is an exact mirror image of the first one? Can you spot it?

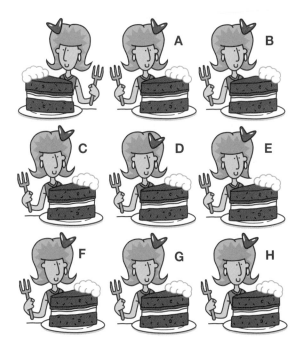

Answer on page 175

Paint by Numbers

Colour in the odd numbers to reveal... What?

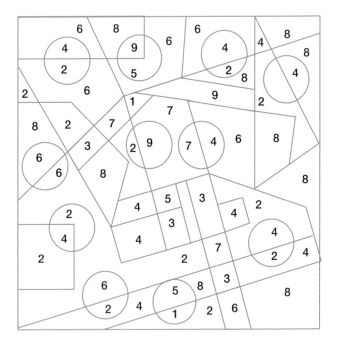

Answer on page 175

Picture Parts

Which box contains exactly the right bits to make the pic?

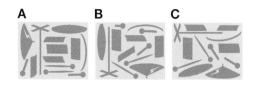

A   B   C

Answer on page 175

Radar

The numbers in some cells in the grid indicate the exact number of black cells that should border it. Shade these black, until all the numbers are surrounded by the correct number of black cells.

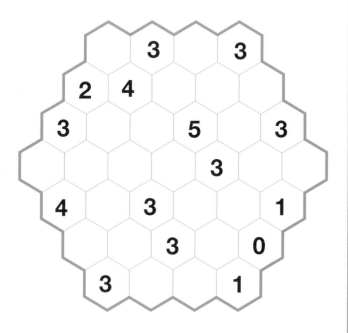

Answer on page 175

Answers

Page 6

Page 7

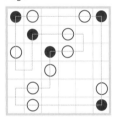

Page 8

Solution: If its bordering triangles are predominantly red, a cell becomes red. If they are predominantly green, it becomes green. If the bordering cells are equal in number, the triangle becomes black

Page 9

Answer: A and C, B and E, H and F, D and G

Page 10

Solution: A line on the top or bottom of this square will only give up one box to your opponent

Page 11

Solution: Each horizontal and vertical line contains two blue phones and a pink one. Each line contains one ringing phone and two that aren't ringing. Each line contains two phones on the hook and one off the hook. Each line contains one pink, one white and one blue dial. The missing image must be a pink phone that isn't ringing, on the hook, and with a white label

Answers

Page 12
Answer: 4 hamsters and 3 cages

Page 13

Page 14
Answer: C and E are the pair

Page 15
Answer: 3.35 am on Wednesday in London; 11.35 pm on Tuesday in Buenos Aires

Page 16

4	7	1	8	5	6	2	9	3
8	6	2	7	9	3	4	1	5
5	9	3	4	1	2	8	7	6
2	5	7	9	6	8	1	3	4
6	8	9	1	3	4	5	2	7
1	3	4	2	7	5	9	6	8
7	1	5	3	8	9	6	4	2
3	4	6	5	2	1	7	8	9
9	2	8	6	4	7	3	5	1

Page 17

1	7	3	4	8	9	5	2	6
6	9	8	1	5	2	4	7	3
4	5	2	6	3	7	1	8	9
3	4	9	2	1	6	8	5	7
5	2	1	9	7	8	6	3	4
7	8	6	5	4	3	2	9	1
2	3	5	7	6	1	9	4	8
9	1	7	8	2	4	3	6	5
8	6	4	3	9	5	7	1	2

Page 18

7	6	4	3	1	8	5	9	2
3	2	9	6	5	4	8	7	1
1	8	5	7	9	2	6	4	3
2	7	8	4	6	9	1	3	5
5	9	1	2	8	3	4	6	7
6	4	3	5	7	1	9	2	8
4	1	6	8	2	7	3	5	9
8	3	7	9	4	5	2	1	6
9	5	2	1	3	6	7	8	4

Page 19

Page 20
It was driven there in winter, when the lake was frozen.

5	2	1	4	6	8	9	7	3
4	6	9	5	7	3	2	8	1
8	3	7	2	1	9	5	4	6
3	1	2	9	4	6	7	5	8
6	8	5	3	2	7	1	9	4
7	9	4	1	8	5	6	3	2
9	5	6	8	3	2	4	1	7
2	4	8	7	5	1	3	6	9
1	7	3	6	9	4	8	2	5

Page 21

0	1	1	0	0	1
0	⇒	⇒	↙	↗	2
0	↗	↑	↓	⇒	1
2	↑	⇐	↗	⇐	0
1	↙	↗	↘	↙	0
0	0	0	1	0	0

Answers

Page 22

Page 23

Page 24
Answer: A

Page 25

Page 26
Solution: C and D

Page 27
Solution below

Page 28
Answer: B. Each row and column in the grid contains four dark and three light squares, and numbers that total 10

Page 29
Answer: Mount Rushmore

Answers

Page 30

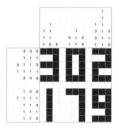

Page 31

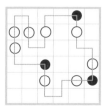

Page 32
Answer: G

Page 33
Answer: I is the odd one out

Page 34

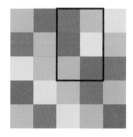

Page 35
Answer: A

Page 36
Answer: B and E are the pair

Page 37
Solution: $22 + 8 \div 5 - 3 = 3$

Answers

Page 38

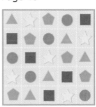

Page 39
Solution: 23

 2

 4

 6

 9

Page 40

Page 41
Answer: D10, I14, L3, K4

Page 42

Page 43
Answer: 18

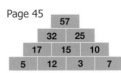

Page 44
Answer: D

Page 45

Answers

Page 46
Answer: B

Page 47
Answer: 37

Page 48
Solution: A line on the left
or bottom of this square will
only give up one box to our
opponent

Page 49

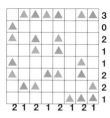

Page 50
Answer: Down

Page 51

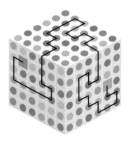

Page 52
Answer: A

Page 53
Answer: E1, N7, C9, J5

Answers

Page 54
Answer: 20 times. 9, 19, 29, 39, 49, 59, 69, 79, 89, 90, 91, 92, 93, 94, 95, 96, 97, 98 and twice in 99.

Page 55
Answer: Yellow

Page 56
Solution: $8 \times 3 \div 6 \times 2 = 8$

Page 57
Answer: C and I are the pair.

Page 58
Solution: a.

Page 59

Page 60
Answer:
5.05 am on Friday in Tokyo
1.05 am on Friday in Karachi

Page 61
Answer:
An orange square with a green circle. Each row and column contains one yellow, two orange and three purple squares, and two pink circles and a green circle.

Answers

Page 62
Solution: 19

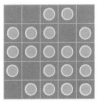

Page 63

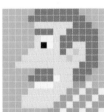

Page 64
Solution below

Page 65
Answer: The Pyramids and the Sphinx

Page 66
Answer: Because nobody knew it was World War One at the time

Page 67
Answer: D

Page 68

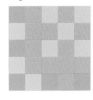

Solution: If its bordering square (not diagonals) are predominantly green, a square becomes green. If they are predominantly yellow it becomes yellow. If the bordering cell colours are equal in number, the square becomes orange and if the bordering squares have now become predominantly orange, a square also becomes orange.

Page 69
Solution: B and F

Answers

Page 70
Solution: Each horizontal and vertical line contains one dog with a white ear.

Each line contains two dogs with a white patched eye.

Each line contains two dogs with their tongues out.

The missing image must have a white patched eye, no white ear, and the tongue out.

Page 71
Answer: D is the odd one out

Page 72
Answer: C

Page 73
Answer: C11, P12, A13, P10

Page 74
Answer: D and H are the pair

Page 75
Solution: 90
The numbers represent the number of sides in the shape they occupy. When shapes overlap, the numbers are added together.
A: $4 + 4 + 3 = 9$
B: $4 + 1 + 5 = 10$
$9 \times 10 = 90$

Page 76
Answer: A, C, G and H, B, D, E and F (The letters are A and B)

Page 77
Answer: 42

Page 78

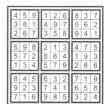

Answers

Page 79
Answer: E and I are the pair

Page 80
Answer: I had put sugar in my tea, and the "new" cup, which should have been unsugared, was sweet!

Page 81
Solution:

Each horizontal and vertical line contains one blue and two yellow dogs.

Each line contains one right-facing and two left-facing dogs.

Each line contains one right-facing and two left-facing crabs.

Each line contains a one-star, a two-star and a three-star picture.

The missing picture must have a left-facing yellow dog, a left-facing crab and two stars.

Page 82
Answer: G

Page 83
Solution: $10 \div 2 \times 4 - 7 = 13$

Page 84
Answer: C and E are the pair.

Page 85

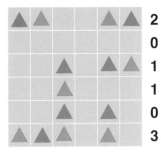

Answers

Page 86
Solution: $14 \times 2 \div 7 + 1 = 5$

Page 87

8	13	6
7	9	11
12	5	10

Page 88
Answer: The Taj Mahal

Page 89
Solution: Each horizontal and vertical line contains one blue, one yellow and one purple man. Each line contains one man with his hands up, one with his hands down and one with his hands stretched out. The missing picture should be of a yellow man with his hands stretched out

Page 90
Answer: B

Page 91
Answer: B

Page 92
Answer: C

Page 93
Answer: I5, K1, M7, J15

Answers

Page 94
Answer: C and G are the pair

Page 95

Page 96
Answer: Let the air out of the truck's tyres

Page 97

Page 98
Solution: A line on the left or right of this square will only give up one box to your opponent

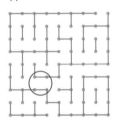

Page 99

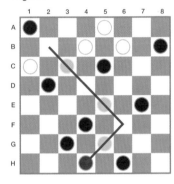

Page 100
Solution: MOZART

L	G	Y	W	R	M
Y	M	G	L	W	R
M	W	R	G	L	Y
W	R	M	Y	G	L
R	L	W	M	Y	G
G	Y	L	R	M	W

4	6	2	1	3	5
3	1	6	2	5	4
5	4	3	6	2	1
6	2	1	5	4	3
2	5	4	3	1	6
1	3	5	4	6	2

G + 6 = M   L + 3 = O
Y + 1 = Z   W + 4 = A
M + 5 = R   R + 2 = T

Page 101
Answer: A and G are the pair

Answers

Page 102
Answer: E and I are the pair

Page 103

8	3	4	2	1	7	5	6	9
2	1	5	3	9	6	4	8	7
6	7	9	4	8	5	1	2	3
1	9	6	5	7	2	3	4	8
7	2	3	1	4	8	9	5	6
4	5	8	6	3	9	7	1	2
5	6	1	9	2	3	8	7	4
9	4	7	8	6	1	2	3	5
3	8	2	7	5	4	6	9	1

Page 104

Page 105

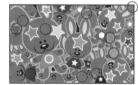

Solution: Each horizontal and vertical line contains one red pencil and two yellow ones. Each line contains one green, one red and one grey symbol. Each line contains two crosses and a tick.

Each line contains one inverted pencil. The missing picture should be a yellow pencil, with a red symbol (which should be a cross) that is not inverted

Page 106
Answer: D

Page 107

1	3	3	4	5	1
4	O	X	X	X	3
2	O	X	O	O	4
3	X	O	O	X	3
4	O	O	X	O	3
1	1	4	3	3	1

Page 108
Answer: Cream

Page 109
Answer: 52% percent is pink, 48% is green. 13 out of 25 squares in the grid are pink, 12 are green. Multiply both numbers by 4 and you see a percentage

Answers

Page 110
Answer: A green square containing a number 2. Each row and column contains three black, two green and one red square, and numbers that total 5

Page 111

Page 112

Page 113
Solution below

Page 114
Answer: a is the odd shape out

Page 115
Solution: Each horizontal and vertical line contains a square, a pentagon and a

triangle. Each line contains one green, one yellow and one blue shape. Each line contains the numbers 1, 2 and 3. Each line contains a black number, a white number and a blue number. The missing picture should be of a green pentagon with a white number 1.

Page 116

Page 117
Answer: B9, H16, N16, G1

170

Answers

Page 118
Answer:
3.30 am on Tuesday in Reykjavic
5.30 am on Tuesday in Cairo

Page 119

B	D	A	C	E	F
D	C	E	A	F	B
E	F	C	D	B	A
A	B	F	E	D	C
C	E	B	F	A	D
F	A	D	B	C	E

Page 120
Solution below

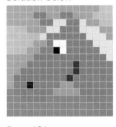

Page 121
Answer: 10 revolutions of
cog A, which will make exactly
15 revolutions of cog B and
12 revolutions of cog C

Page 122

Page 123
Answer: E is the odd one out

Page 124

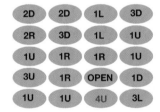

Page 125
Answer: 15
Multiply the number of letters in
the name of each city by three,
and subtract 1 for each vowel
18 − 3 = 15

Answers

Page 126
Solution: Each horizontal and vertical line contains the letters A, B and C. Each line contains two pink letters and a green letter. Each line contains two asterisks and one circle. The missing picture should be of a pink letter A with a circle

Page 127

Page 128

7	6	8	7	6	8	9	8	9	9	8	8
8	7	7	6	7	7	6	6	6	6	6	6
8	8	7	8	8	9	8	9	8	8	9	9
9	7	7	8	8	8	9	7	9	7	8	8
6	6	8	6	7	7	7	8	7	9	7	7
8	9	8	7	8	9	8	9	8	8	7	9
9	8	7	8	9	8	9	6	6	9	8	6
7	8	9	7	6	6	6	8	9	6	6	8
8	6	8	9	8	9	8	9	8	8	9	9
9	9	6	6	9	8	9	8	7	6	7	7
6	7	9	8	6	6	7	8	7	9	8	8
8	9	7	9	8	9	8	9	6	8	9	6

Page 129
Answer: A, B and D

Page 130
Solution: $9 - 2 \times 2 + 6 = 20$

Page 131
Answer:
A) 6 – Add opposite numbers and multiply the integers of the total
B) 12 – Multiply the opposite numbers, then multiply the integers of the total

Page 132

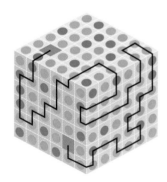

Page 133
Answer : B

Answers

Page 134

Page 135
Answer: B and H are the pair

Page 136
Solution: 17

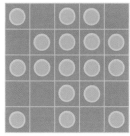

Page 137
Answer: A = 20 and B = 160
The numbers represent the number of sides in the shape they occupy. When shapes overlap, the numbers are multiplied. 5 x 4 x 1 = 20 and 4 x 4 x 10 = 160

Page 138

2	1	4	3	5	6
1	4	6	2	3	5
3	6	5	1	2	4
5	3	2	6	4	1
6	5	3	4	1	2
4	2	1	5	6	3

Page 139
Answer:
blue 1   yellow 2
red 3   green 4

Page 140

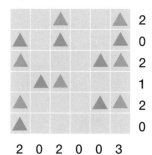

Page 141
Answer: Lunchalot is knight H

Answers

Page 142
Answer: D. Each row and column in the grid contains two red squares and a black triangle, and numbers that total 9

Page 143
Answer: 4

Page 144
Solution: C and E

Page 145
Solution: Each horizontal and vertical line contains two square shapes and one diamond shape. Each line contains one green, one blue and one white central square. Each line contains two red asterisks. The missing image should be a square shape containing a blue square with no asterisk

Page 146

1	2	5 >	3	4
3 ^	4 ^ >	1	2 ˇ	5 ^
2 ˇ	3	4 <	5	1
5	1	2 <	4 ˇ	3 ^
4 <	5	3 >	1	2

Page 147

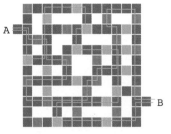

Page 148
Answer: A

Page 149

A

B

Answers

Page 150

Page 151
Solution: C

Page 152

Page 153
Answer: G

Page 154
Solution: A Footballer

Page 155
Answer: C

Page 156

Your puzzle notes